REFLECTIONS

A Collection of 5-Minute Essays

UMA RAJAGOPAL

INDIA · SINGAPORE · MALAYSIA

ISBN 979-8-88883-633-0

I dedicate this book to my daughter
D.U.Tejashri.

Contents

Acknowledgement

I would like to thank my elder sister Renuka Rajagopal and my close friends B. VijayBabu and Shymala T S who encouraged me to write a book and stood with me during hard times.

I also thank my parents for supporting me morally.

It is like a dream come true for me.

Whole-heartedly, I would like to thank my publisher for accepting my idea and providing me a platform.

Be the best version of yourself

Uma Rajagopal

Behind Every Successful Mom There is her Kid

Hi all,

I wrote this a night before my kid was born.

Every Woman is special in her own way. Motherhood adds a crown to a woman. Motherhood shapes a woman in positive ways and brings the best out of her.

I would like to share my experience.

One day my manager told in stand up that there is an opening for the position of Product Owner. I didn't take it that seriously, because I doubted my capability, I felt I would not be suitable for the role though I was very much interested in it.

But next day while riding my scooty, something within me, not my conscience that is for sure, something else within me was telling me "You should give it a try and you can do it".

I was wondering from where this unusual confidence came from, its definitely not me.

Within few weeks an interview was scheduled and I faced it confidently. It was an unusual confidence I had and I was sure I will clear it. I cleared the interview. There was a constant positive energy driving me and supporting me throughout the interview.

That weekend all of sudden I felt very tired and was taken to doctor. Doctor did my scan and confirmed my pregnancy, I heard the heartbeat of my kid for first time. I got the answer to my question from where I got this confidence from, all of sudden.

If we apply science to what I felt, it will not look logical and would sound stupid. But I truly felt a positive change within me.

Usually people will say, we should be happy always and control our anger, keep ourselves away from negative thoughts. We tend to ignore all these simple, yet powerful advises.

Whenever I was angry or sad about something, my baby's kick was like a gatekeeper telling me that "you should not allow negative thoughts to enter into your mind, if you want me to be healthy".

Immediately, I had to replace them with positive thoughts. I had to learn techniques to keep myself happy and avoid getting angry.

My kid was growing and changing me, purifying me, making me a better person every day.

For you my kid:

==============

I have not touched you, seen you, all I can do is to feel you. But I am curious and excited to meet the person who has changed me so much. Who has been constantly reminding me that I should be taking every decision of mine whether professional or personal with boldness, confidence, honesty, truthfulness because "I am watching you".

You can cheat your subconscious mind, but not the kid who is listening to you all the time.

Time to Discover 'U'

One of the most beautiful creation of god is woman. Born with the skill of multitasking . Every woman is beautiful in her own way . We should be proud that we can handle so many tasks so effortlessly.

A woman cooks, takes care of kids, keeps home neat, packs food for their family, helps her kid in their homework...the list is endless. But still reaches office on time and performs her work with full commitment.

Majority of us fall into this category, which is good. But we should push ourselves a little bit and move a little further. We should discover what our passion is and give some time for it as well.

I keep asking my friends what they are passionate about?

Some say they like dancing, some say singing, some say writing and some playing the guitar.

Then my immediate question will be, why don't they do it ?

The common complaint is lack of time and energy. This is a challenge even I am facing. I like dancing, especially classical dance. Believe me how much ever stressful my day be, if I dance for some time,it relives me from stress and makes me happy.

It was my dream to get dressed in Bharatnatyam attire and get a nice photo of mine and hang it in the centre of my living room. It was just a dream and never executed. One day I was listening to "Mahaganapatim song" during lunch break. I liked that song so much and decided I will dance for this song whenever I will get a chance. I was waiting for a platform to perform. After 4 months got an email from fun committee that our company was going to celebrate annual day. Immediately I send my name saying "I would like to perform Bharatnatyam dance". I learnt dance for 1 year only.

So I was underestimating my capability.

In the evening, I went home and was asking myself questions like "Uma, you danced in

5th standard only, now after so many years you are going to dance again? Are you sure the audience will like it? What if you forget your steps while dancing and freeze on stage?". Every negative thought was replaced by only one vision of mine. "Imagining a beautiful photo of mine in Bharatnatyam dress in my living room." I decided for sure I will dance. I practised almost for 1 week, morning 1 hour before going to office and evening one hour after returning from office. Finally annual day came. When my name was announced, I just assured myself only one thing "Don't worry about forgetting steps, do not worry about audience, just listen to the lyrics of the song and keep going." It came out so beautiful and every one appreciated me so much. I can never forget that happiest day in my life.

There is no one stopping us from following our passion, except our own mental block. It is very important to keep ourselves happy. If we are stressed out, how can we spread happiness to all. We give time to everyone around us, but we forget to give time for our self.

I want to keep this article simple and small. Jump, dance, sing, do something crazy everyday.

We don't own all problems. Give some time for your happiness everyday. Pick up some hobby. Do not allow that smile to disappear from your face. It's time to Discover 'U

Who is Your Role Model?

In my childhood days, when people used to ask me the question "Who is your role model"?

I used to give so many names. They are the people who are legends in different fields and some are noble prize winners.

Two days back, I googled to find out the meaning of "Role model". Here is what Google says "a person looked to by others as an example to be imitated".

Now I paused and tried to find an answer to same old question, "Who is your role model?".

Every human being is unique and special in their own way, do we really need to imitate some one? Can we truly successfully imitate some one?

For me, the answer to the above questions is certainly no. Then **Who is my role model?**

I saw myself in the mirror and got the answer. It is me ☺ ☺. I am here to evolve, grow and be the best version of myself ☺.

Happy Women's day to all wonderful ladies. You are unique and you are here to deliver the best version of yourself and not to imitate anyone.

Believe in yourself!!

Does Motherhood Mean Sacrifice?

Many times I have heard people saying that motherhood means sacrifice. "Your kid should be your only focus and your dreams should revolve around your kid".

A woman makes a lot of sacrifices. But believe me, motherhood does not mean sacrifice.

It is enjoying your dreams and working towards your happiness. The moment kids sees the mother enjoying her life to fullest, they will see life from a different perspective.

Kids observe everything and learn from it. Let us not portray an image that motherhood means sacrificing and leaving one's own dream.

It is actually the other way, the more successful and cheerful a mother is, she spreads the positive energy which is absorbed by the kid and is reflected back. Let us fly together and enjoy motherhood.

Motherhood does not mean sacrifices.

Motherhood means **celebrations.**

Are You Truly Independent?

Just before a day, India was ready to celebrate it's 75th Independence day. I stepped out of home and went till N.S.C Bose road. The whole Chennai was decorated with lights. All the government offices in Anna Salai was glowing with serial lights. It was looking like a big festival all over. I went through the same road many times, but only that day I saw happiness in everyone's face, whomever I could see from auto. May be because I was so excited to celebrate Independence day and I was very happy, I could see only happiness all around me.

The next day, I got up early and took my little daughter to the nearby school to see the flag hoisting. I was explaining her about Tricolor, significance of each color, and about the national anthem. After noon, when she was sleeping, I decided to go for a ride and enjoy some **Me time**. I was riding through a flyover near Chennai Airport. I saw a big Indian flag was hoisted in airport. The flag was gently but majestically waiving in the sky.

I started thinking "How much struggle our ancestors have gone through to get this Independence for us. Many have sacrificed their life and many lost their family to make India Independent."

Independence is the biggest blessing. In one of tamil movie song lyrics it is said that "Even if we are in heaven and not independent, there is absolutely no use of being in heaven." I like that lyrics and everyone would agree that it as an ultimate truth.

Have you ever seen when a cage is opened for a bird, it just flies up. It just feels liberated and just flies flapping its wings. But we human beings, we are prisoners of our own self created fear. Self-doubt, low self esteem, self created fear is like a self created cage which will never allow us to fly.

Let us break this self created cage and fly up in sky and enjoy the freedom given to us. That is when we will be truly liberated.

Twinkle, Twinkle Little Star

This Diwali(2022), I remembered this song which I used to sing in my childhood days "Twinkle, Twinkle, little star …"

But this time when I was humming this song, it was totally different gleam. I avoided firing crackers, but I like to see kids bursting crackers. All the kids were bursting crackers and I could see colorful rockets hitting the sky. Different colors(red, green, yellow) of rockets which were bursting out in the sky. It was beautiful to see. Colors from the rockets lasted only for few seconds and it turned into smoke and was slowly disappearing. Black color smoke was floating in sky and then slowly mingled along with black clouds.

After the smoke disappeared, all I could see in the black sky was the twinkling star. The star remained in the same place, its brightness was the same and it was twinkling with the same intensity and was looking like a small diamond in the black sky.

There was a spiritual message this tiny little twinkling star was conveying me. If you remain calm, stable and twinkling and not bursting, you will not disappear as a smoke. People will see this twinkling star in the dark cloud. Your presence and beauty can never go unnoticed.

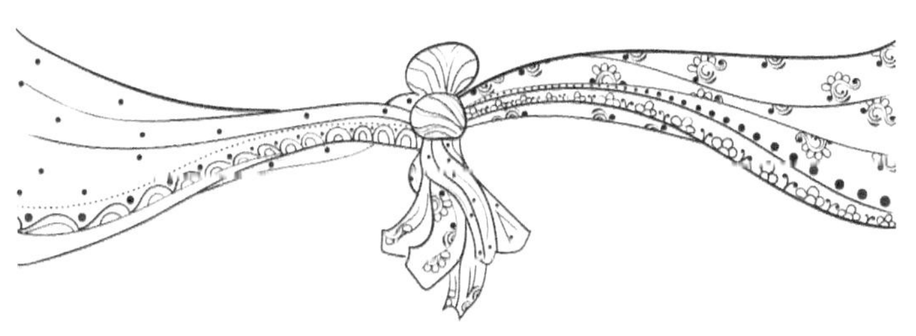

Why it is called Better Half?

It always triggers my brain cells, when people use some special words. One such word is better-half.

Many times when a spouse introduce their life partner, they say "he/she is my better half".

Why it is called "better-half"? Why not "best-half". Can a marriage or relationship bring more prosperity and make you flourish? The answer is "Yes", provided you both are compatible. Your life can be better than what it is, if you are with the right person. Still to make your life the best experience, it is only you who can do that.

It is only you who can make entire journey of your life beautiful. Whether you have a "better-half" or not, that is not what I am focusing on. At any given situation only you can bring the best version of yourself.

Be the best version of yourself, that is the very purpose of your creation.

Only you know what makes you happy, what your dreams are. Only you know how to make your **whole life and not just half of your life** beautiful.

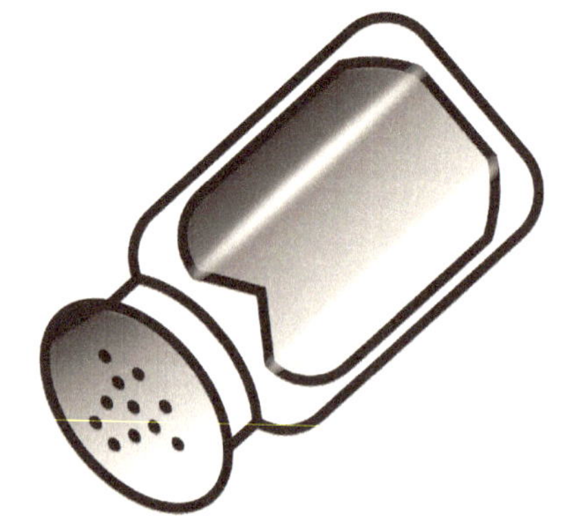

Saltless Restaurant

My elder sister is a doctor and she keeps saying one thing "High BP and diabetics are silent killers".They themselves are not disease, but can affect every organ of the body. Majority of the population is affected either by one/both of these silent killers. Actually it is not tough to control both of them, if we become little conscious.

I am a hypertension patient. My bp always used to be 140/95 even after taking tablets. I was really frustrated with this reading. I tried walking. After walking for 30 minutes daily, I saw my bp reduced by 5 points, still not within normal range. I started doing meditation for 5-10 minutes, it reduced my BP by 5 points. Definitely some improvements, but very significant change.

Finally I reduced my salt intake and saw miracle started happening. My BP reduced by 20 points in a week. From that time I reduced my salt intake.

There was a camp going on in a near by hospital for heart test. EGC, thread mill test and echo test all three tests and free cardiologist appointment, this entire package for a very minimal charge. I decided to go for this test. I completed my echo, EGC. Nurse took my BP before and after threadmill test and were gossiping while writing my BP reading. Out of curiosity I asked "Can I know my BP?".

She said even after running in threadmill, your BP is within normal range only. Nurse said " you can leave today and come tomorrow. You can collect your report as well as meet cardiologist."

Next day I went to hospital and met cardiologist. He saw my reports and said all reports are normal. Asked "Do you have any problem and any medication you are taking for it?". I said " I have BP for past 4 years and I am taking BP tablets". He checked my BP and wrote on my report "Asymptotic". He reduced dosage of my tablet by half. He said "just follow your routine and come after 3 months, if everything is fine, I will remove tablets itself".

I was in cloud seven. A small conscious effort has yielded a big result for me. I really wanted to celebrate this victory over silent killer. I went to hospital canteen. I love Ginger tea. So, I decided to celebrate this happiness with ginger tea. I ordered for tea. While collecting tea from counter, the person in counter asked "with sugar or without sugar?", I said "with Sugar". Next question "one spoon or two spoon?" I like to add lot of sugar to my tea, but to look decent I told "1.5 spoon". With each sip of ginger tea, I was enjoying my victory.

But immediately a thought came "world is so much aware of the ill effects of sugar and steps are taken even at a small tea shop to fight diabetes. Such awareness does not exist for BP".

Salt and it association with BP should also be injected into people's mind. Restaurant should be providing options like:

No salt.

Less salt.

Normal salt.

Less Luggage, More Comfortable

My father got transferred from Chennai to Gujarat. So we had to shift along with him. We moved to Gujarat when I was in 5th standard. We used to come to our native place only during summer vacation. Me and my elder sister used to wait the whole year for summer vacation. Getting a confirmed ticket was a very big thing because we had to go to ticket counter to get the booking done, no internet facility during those days. Next thing after getting confimed ticket is fight that who will sit near window seat. If we get two window seat that is great. Otherwise me and my sister had to do some adjustments and come to agreement about sharing window seat.

The biggest task was packing bags. Before one month itself we would start our packing. By the time we are ready for travelling, it would be almost 16-20 bags(excluding food and water).

It is 36 hours journey in train from Gujarat to Chennai.

Getting a coolie, bargaining for money to place these luggages in compartment was a usual problem which my parents had to handle.

There is a maximum limit of weight which each person can carry, many times we exceeded that limit and had to pay extra charges as penalty. This is not the end of the problem, finding place for keeping the luggage is another very big problem altogether.

Many of the luggages would be placed in the upper berth and I used to be asked to sleep in the upper berth. Since I am a little short in height, I could fit into that small place.

In railway coaches it would be written "Less Luggage, more comfortable". If we just carried what was essential and did not pack unnecessary things, how pleasant the journey would be? In life also it is true, just carry what is essential, otherwise our own baggage will become a big burden to carry and will not allow us to enjoy this journey called "LIFE".

God is Supporting Library

Whenever I discuss with my team about any new project and creating new executables, immediately they will say "Uma we have to identify supporting libraries and integrate it to our application". Those who are from engineering background will know that libraries are not executables, they cannot run on their own. Executable can run, but they need libraries.

I saw a deep spiritual message conveyed to me during one such discussion where we were talking about creating new executables. I can connect this with my understanding about God. God is supporting library, our goals and vision are executables.

When we choose the right set of libraries and build our executables, you think we will ever fail?

When our goals are clear and get that little push from god, what we create out of this combination is always beautiful and will definitely bring contentment to our life.

Who Owns the Unknown?

On 12 Aug 2022, my father got a major heart attack and he was hospitalized. The doctor called me and told "Uma your father is in a very critical stage and needs immediate surgery. Anything can happen even during surgery. It is a high risk surgery. 10% risk is always there for any surgery. Your father's life is already at very high risk. Surgery will take almost 6 hours to complete. I will try my best". He looked like a very senior surgeon. I wished all these things happening around me was some bad dream and not a reality. For a second I was completely blank. I thought I should not be emotional rather stay strong. When this very positive thought came to me, I asked doctor "Can you tell me surgery charges" and I did not ask any other question. No point in asking any other questions because there was no other option.

Doctor said "If you want to talk to your father, you can talk, but do not get emotional in front of him". I went inside the room, I said to my dad "You will be discharged soon, do not worry". Gave thumbs up to him and came out of room.

In life also many times we are not left with many options. There is no point in analysing and thinking too much in such situations. Over thinking will never help. Accepting reality and making the first move in the right direction according to our conscience is the only choice we have. Just trust that "Unknown" is owned by supreme power and that supreme power will always work in our favor.

Supreme power will definitely work in our favour as long as we believe in it strongly. You should not doubt your decisions. I strongly held the belief that my father will come out of surgery successfully. I delegated "Unknown" to god.

RIP

Couple of days back one of my school teacher passed away. Everyone started texting "RIP" in our WhatsApp school group. Even I texted "RIP" in that group. But this time I did not stop after texting "RIP", I paused and started thinking what "RIP" means? When someone is dead, why we say "RIP"?

"RIP" means "Rest In Peace". "Peace" means calm and composed. Can you "Rest In Peace", if you have not "Lived In Peace"? You cannot die, remain calm and composed, if you have not lived your life full-fledged.

Another incident was, I was returning from Pallavaram in an auto-rickshaw and saw a dead body being carried in a "Golden chariot". The chariot was decorated with lot of beautiful and colorful flowers. I derived a beautiful message from these incidents.

It does not matter whether your final journey happens in a "Golden Chariot" or not. What matters is whether the entire journey called life is beautiful, colorful and a fulfilling one.

Both these converged at one point. You can automatically RIP if you have LIP. If you have accomplished your dreams and lived your life to fullest, you will automatically "RIP".

"LIP" leads to "RIP".

Two Sides of the Ocean

Rameshwaram is a very beautiful place. It is located at the tip of India. Anyone who went for a drive from Rameshwaram to Dhanuskodi can never forget the experience. It is just a 16 Kms drive, but a memorable one. Sangamam at Dhanushkodi is a place for those who want to admire the creator of universe.

While driving from Rameshwaram to Dhanukodi, you can see sea water on both the sides of the road.

On one side it is turbulent sea waves and another side it is almost still water. I could not believe my own eyes. I looked left and right many times to confirm that what I am seeing and feeling is a reality and not an illusion. How can two drastically different characteristic of ocean can exist at same place.

You can also see both these merge at one point, that is called Sangamam.

I was asking myself "did you like the turbulent side or the silent side of ocean"?

Almost still water resembled to me like a huge saint doing meditation and finding peace within himself.

Turbulent side resembled a highly energetic and strong willed person constantly working towards his goal. The force at which it splashed on the rocks looked like someone bouncing back with tremendous energy and emerging successful.

It is a very rare combination, but if it can co-exist and converge at one point, then everything is achievable.

To me both sides of the ocean were beautiful, but the most beautiful thing was convergence. A deep spiritual message I carried from this place.

Sand-Timer

New year means new resolutions. Every new year I used to prepare a list of resolutions. One of them was of walking half an hour. I used to follow them for few weeks and then leave. But for 2022 New year, I gifted myself a meaningful and life changing gift.

I ordered for myself a sand timer. It is a 5 minute timer filled with pink color sand. Sand timer is very small, but indeed brought a huge positive change in my life. I have placed it near my printer, so that I can see it quite often. It fed this message deep into my mind that "life is short and colorful". We have absolutely no time to waste our life in unnecessary things. The moment mind understands this, blue print to achieve what is essential in your life is laid by it. The life clock is always tinkling down. Life is short, so keep it simple. Do not complicate life by wavering thoughts, negative people, grudges, revenge. Just focus on what is essential. Only essential thing to do in life is to live happily and remove weeds from life.

When you understand this simple reality, no need of big master plans or things like that. You will automatically be taking only right steps.

The biggest gift of your life is "YOU".

Where is God?

I learned a lot from my 3-year-old daughter. She is one person who has brought a lot of positive change in me.

I do not need to allocate time for exercise separately in my schedule. Simply running after her itself would aptly fall under the category of moderate exercise. I have not gained weight since she was born.

She is the one who taught me how to control my anger. If I get angry, she will say "Amma smile, kovama irrukadha".

"Mom smile, do not be angry". Have you ever tried this technique? When you are extremely angry, just try to smile. Believe me, it provides instant relief and you won't be holding onto the feeling of anger for long.

Whenever I get time on weekdays, I take her to the Sai Baba temple near my house. Just opposite the sandwich shop, there is a temple, where we both often go after visiting the temple and seeking blessings of the deity. We order sandwiches and smileys. She likes smiley a lot.

We have Sai Baba's photo at our home. Looking at the photo, my daughter said "Sai Baba is at our home and he is also in the temple". I was astonished listening to it. I stood completely frozen when a small kid made me realize this universal truth.

God is everywhere and not just in religious places.

I Want to Share *Bhajji*

I take my daughter to Besant Nagar beach on weekends. She likes to collect sea shells and play in the mud. Usually, she will find some kids of her age on the beach and will start playing with them. Kids have very good socializing skills, we just have to encourage them to cultivate it. While she was playing, I thought of buying *bhajji* for my parents. *Bhajji* and *sundal* is a popular Chennai beach snack, a favorite for those who visit beaches in Chennai. Seeing me going to buy *bhajji*, my daughter also joined me.

While we were waiting for the hot *bhajji* to be prepared, I saw a family sitting and having *bhajji*. A one-year kid was sitting on her mother's lap. Her mother gave a piece of *bhajji* to her. Immediately, the small kid grabbed that piece of *bhajji* and waved at my daughter. She wanted to share it with my daughter. No one asked her to share.

Kids are so innocent and their love is pure. They do not need any language to communicate their thought. They just smile and get the attention of people. A smiling kid is the epitome of positivity. We, adults, have forgotten to smile and share. Even if you do not have anything, just share your smile. A smile costs nothing, but will make a big difference in how you feel as well as to the people around you.

A Squirrel Climbed a Coconut Tree

Mandous cycle had hit Chennai and it was raining heavily. I was in one of the rooms in our terrace, attending an office meeting. It is at that time, I started hearing a squirrel squeaking continuously. I was in an important meeting, so I could not get up to check what made the squirrel squeak so much. Almost after half an hour, I got up and saw that the squirrel had gotten trapped in a rat trap. Seeing me it got even more scared, as though I were going to kill it. I was a little scared myself. I was apprehensive about the possibility of the squirrel biting me while opening the rat trap. Finally, we both came to an understanding as though we both read each other's minds and heard each other's inner voices.

The squirrel went to the end of the rat trap and I somehow got the courage to open the rat trap. Immediately it jumped out. First jump, it was out of the rat trap. Second jump, it was on the fence. Third jump, it was on the coconut tree and disappeared. I felt so happy to see it jumping.

That squirrel knew the value of life. The moment it got an opportunity to survive, it felt relieved and found its own path. But we human beings, fail to accept even small failures and set-backs, and try committing suicide.

One set back, one failure should not define life. The battle is not over yet. Just bounce back and face every challenge life throws at you in an ethical way.

Even in a boxing field, the empire gives you a chance and the time to bounce back. Just trust god and face every battle of your life. One single failure cannot make you a loser.

Life is precious and the battle is not over yet!!

Diet Chart for the Mind

Striking a balance between work and life became extremely difficult for me during the pandemic situation with a one-year-old kid. I was becoming inefficient and was not able to manage anything.

I was in a constant state of unhappiness and lost my peace of mind. It is easy to say, "You should stay calm, be relaxed, keep smiling, control your anger and so on". But I could not execute any of these.

One day I got up by 5 AM and had ample amount of time. I did not know what to do. I thought let me start my day with a cup of tea. I prepared ginger tea and opened the main door. With a hot tea cup in hand and cool fresh air gently touching my cheeks, I moved to a happy state. With each sip, I felt so lively and so fresh. This routine continued for almost a week. Still, I had 45 min and was not knowing what to do.

I saw a motivational book lying on my rack. I picked it up and started reading it just for 15 min every day. Taking 15 minutes out of 24 hours was not a big deal. Slowly I started enjoying reading, sometimes I used to read for 1 hour also. Reading changed me a lot. Starting a day in a positive way is really very important.

Even after all this, I had a good amount of time left. So I picked up my office laptop and quickly went through all emails (especially long ones and prepared notes for upcoming meetings. It was another 15 minutes. Slowly that also became a habit for me. 15 minutes of preparation was so helpful and reduced my stress.

Still, another 15 mins was left. In that 15 min, I decided not to do anything. Just used to watch the rising sun, the humming birds, the colorful butterflies and the blooming flowers. I was connecting with nature.

I started following this 1 hour of self-created diet chart. This diet chart was not enforced on me. I follow it because I love it. This became my habit itself and everything started falling into place.

There is no single formula that can be applied to all. But just start with 15 min. Like physical body, mind needs to be taken care of. A healthy diet for the mind is equally important. Diet for the mind cannot be prepared by someone else. You have to hunt for it, customize it for yourself and feed it at the right time, with the right dosage.

The mind too needs a healthy diet.